BELIZE

ONDURAS

NICARA

OSTA RICA

# CENTRAL AMERICA

## ANITA GANERI AND NICOLA BARBER

A⁺
**Smart Apple Media**

First published in 2004 by Franklin Watts
96 Leonard Street, London EC2A 4XD

Franklin Watts Australia
45-51 Huntley Street, Alexandria NSW 2015

Designer: Steve Prosser, Text Editor: Belinda Hollyer, Art Director: Jonathan Hair, Editor-in-Chief: John C. Miles, Picture Research: Diana Morris, Map Artwork: Ian Thompson

Picture credits
AKG Images: 12
AP/Topham: 23t
Archivo Iconografico, S.A./Corbis: 14
Gustavo Benitez/Presidency/Reuters/Corbis: 23c
Bettmann/Corbis: 15, 17t, 17b, 36
Wesley Bocxe/Image Works/Topham: 20
Bob Daemmrich/Image Works/Topham: 24
Nigel Dickinson/Still Pictures: 27
Mary Evans PL: 28, 29
Luis Galdamez/Reuters/Corbis: 41
Jeff Greenberg/Image Works/Topham: 34
John Mitchell/Image Works/Topham:
front cover t, 9
Fernando Moleres/Sipa Press/Rex Features: 40
Picturepoint/Topham: 13, 25
Popperfoto: 37
Reuters/Corbis: 39
Oswaldo Rivas/Reuters/Corbis: 33
Jorgen Schytte/Still Pictures: 32
Adrian Sherratt/Rex Features: 11
Sipa Press/Rex Features: front cover b, back cover, 19, 21, 22, 26, 30, 31, 35, 38
UPI/Popperfoto: 18

Published in the United States by Smart Apple Media
2140 Howard Drive West, North Mankato, Minnesota 56003

Library of Congress Cataloging-in-Publication Data

Ganeri, Anita, 1961-
Central America / by Anita Ganeri and Nicola Barber.
p. cm. — (Flashpoints)
Includes index.
ISBN 1-58340-609-3
1. Central America—History—Juvenile literature. I. Barber, Nicola. II. Title. III. Flashpoints (Smart Apple Media)

F1428.5.G36 2005
972.8—dc22                     2005043078

9 8 7 6 5 4 3 2 1

# CONTENTS

# INTRODUCTION

**C**entral America is a narrow bridge of land that joins North and South America. The region is made up of seven countries—Belize, Costa Rica, El Salvador, Guatemala, Honduras, Nicaragua, and Panama.

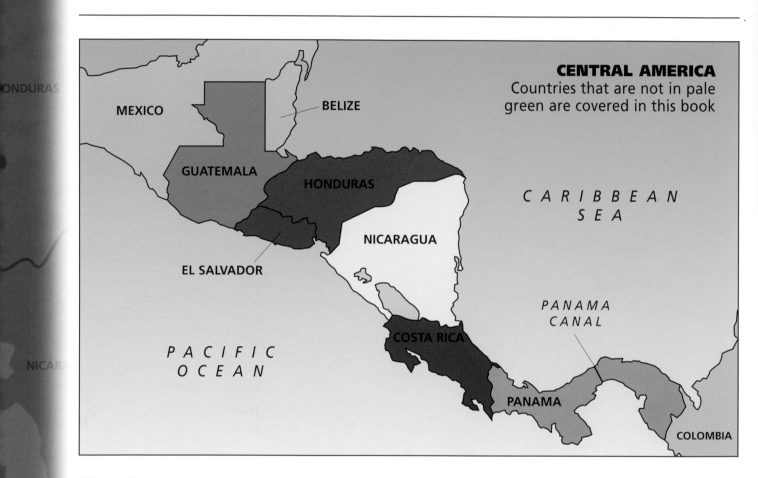

**CENTRAL AMERICA**
Countries that are not in pale green are covered in this book

MEXICO

BELIZE

GUATEMALA

HONDURAS

EL SALVADOR

NICARAGUA

CARIBBEAN SEA

PANAMA CANAL

PACIFIC OCEAN

COSTA RICA

PANAMA

COLOMBIA

### THE LANDSCAPE

Central America has a northern border with Mexico and a southern border with Colombia. To the west lies the Pacific Ocean, and to the east are the Caribbean Sea and the Atlantic Ocean. Most of the coastal land is low-lying and covered in thick jungle, but inland Central America is crossed by high mountain ranges. Many of the mountains in these ranges are volcanoes, and some are still active.

The region is frequently hit by natural disasters, such as violent earthquakes and huge tropical storms that sweep in from August to October, destroying everything in their path.

### THE PANAMA CANAL

The narrowest part of the Central American isthmus is in Panama, the southernmost country in the region. It is here that the Panama Canal was built in the early 20th century so ships could pass between the Caribbean Sea and the Gulf of Panama. The canal meant that ships no longer had to sail around the southern tip of South America to travel between the Atlantic and Pacific Oceans. It shortened this journey by thousands of miles.

## THE REGION'S PEOPLES

Before the Spanish arrived in the 16th century (see pages 12-13), Central America was home to many different groups of American Indians. Today, the population of the region is much more varied. The country with the largest Indian population is Guatemala, at about 60 percent. These people are descended from the ancient Maya, who built a highly developed civilization in the northern part of Central America (see pages 10-11). Other countries in the region, such as Honduras, Nicaragua,

*The Panama Canal is a vital shipping link between the Caribbean Sea and the Pacific Ocean.*

and El Salvador, have mostly "mestizo" populations—people of mixed Indian and European ancestry. Belize and Panama both have large black populations, descended from the black Africans who originally came as slaves or laborers to work on plantations or construction projects.

## TURBULENCE AND POVERTY

Since gaining their independence in the early 19th century, most of the countries of Central America—aside from Belize and Costa Rica—have had turbulent histories. Frequent changes of government, brutal civil wars, and ruthless dictatorships have often brought terrible abuses of human rights. Another constant factor has been the involvement of the United States in the region's politics. There is now greater political stability than ever before, but poverty is still a huge problem, and Nicaragua and Honduras are still among the world's poorest countries.

### A QUESTION OF LANGUAGE

Spanish is the official language of all of the Central American countries except Belize, where the official language is English. Both Spanish and English are widely spoken across the whole region, and there are many other indigenous languages as well. In Guatemala, for example, more than 20 different languages are spoken by the Indian population.

# EARLY HISTORY

**A**round 20,000 years ago, an Ice Age gripped the planet. Huge amounts of water were trapped in ice sheets, which lowered sea levels and exposed land previously covered by oceans. One of these areas of land formed a bridge between Siberia in northern Asia and Alaska in North America. This bridge, now covered by water, is called the Bering Strait.

## EARLY SETTLEMENT

It is thought that people began to cross the Bering Strait land bridge from Asia to the Americas about 15,000 years ago. These people lived by hunting animals and gathering food, and they gradually moved south through the region. As farming developed, some people began to settle permanently in one place. After about 5000 B.C., people in Mesoamerica grew crops such as maize, squash, and beans, as well as chili peppers and avocados. At the same time, they started to produce pottery for cooking and storing food. Permanent villages were established.

## THE MAYA

The best known of all the Indian groups of Mesoamerica is the Maya. From about A.D. 300 until 900 (the Classic period), Mayan was the dominant culture in the region. During this time, Mayan civilization spread across present-day Guatemala and Belize, the southern part of Mexico, and parts of El Salvador and Honduras. It was based around powerful city-states, which had large cities that were built as administrative and ceremonial centers. The remains of these cities still stand today in places such as Tik'al in Guatemala and Copan in Honduras.

At the peak of Mayan civilization, it is likely that cities such as Tik'al had larger populations than any similar settlements in Europe at the time. At the heart of the

### NUMBERS, CALENDARS, AND CALCULATIONS

The Mayans developed a writing system using hieroglyphics and were skilled mathematicians and astronomers. Their number system was based on units of 20, and they kept several calendars. One of these calendars, called the "Long Count," measured time from a particular starting point. Calculated from dates inscribed on Mayan monuments, the starting point is now reckoned to be 3114 B.C.

Mayan cities were huge pyramids topped with temples and large "palaces" that were probably used as administrative centers. These stone buildings were highly decorated with carvings and were brightly painted inside and out. Ordinary homes were made from wood and thatch.

After about 800 A.D., Mayan civilization began to collapse. There were probably several reasons for this, including war between rival city-states, severe droughts that caused food shortages, and overpopulation in some areas. Many cities, including Tik'al, were abandoned. Invaders from Mexico, called the Toltecs, introduced their own religious beliefs and way of life to the Yucatan (the northern region of the old Mayan civilization). But in the south, some Mayan centers continued to flourish until the arrival of the Spanish in the 16th century.

*The Mayans built huge stone pyramids. This is the Temple of the Jaguar at Tik'al, Guatemala.*

## THE INDIANS

To the south of the mighty Mayan civilization, many smaller groups of Indians flourished in Central America. One group, called the Chorotegas, migrated from Mexico to the region of present-day Nicaragua around A.D. 800. The Chorotegas were later partly replaced by the Nicaraguans, who arrived in about 1200 and established a successful trading culture. Farther south, a group called the Corobici lived in the northern part of present-day Costa Rica, while the Boruca lived in the south.

**EARLY HISTORY**

**c. 6000–2000 B.C.**
Archaic period

**c. 2000–1000 B.C.**
Early Pre-Classic period
in Mayan history

**c. 1000–300 B.C.** Middle
Pre-Classic period in
Mayan history

**c. 300 B.C.–A.D. 250**
Late Pre-Classic period
in Mayan history

**c. 300–900** Classic
period in Mayan
history

**c. 800** Chorotegas
migrate south from
Mexico to Nicaragua

**c. 900–1500s** Post-
Classic period in
Mayan history

**c. 1200** Nicaraguans
migrate south from
Mexico to Nicaragua

# THE COLONIAL PERIOD

**I**n 1492, an Italian sailor named Christopher Columbus set sail from Spain. Columbus was employed by King Ferdinand and Queen Isabella of Spain to sail west across the Atlantic Ocean to look for a sea route to the Indies.

Columbus landed in the Caribbean and thought he had found the "Indies." When he returned to Spain with news of his discoveries, which included gold, his voyage opened the floodgates for Spanish adventurers ("conquistadors"). The exploration and exploitation of the Americas by Europeans had begun.

## PANAMA

Columbus himself made three more voyages to the "New World." On his fourth and final expedition, still looking for a route to mainland Asia, he sailed down the coast of Central America from Honduras toward Panama. Exploration of the mainland, however, did not begin until Spanish conquistadors Pedrarias Davila and Vasco Nunez de Balboa led expeditions to Panama. In 1513, Balboa became the first European to see the Pacific Ocean when his expedition crossed the Panamanian isthmus. Balboa claimed the land for Spain. In 1519, Davila founded Panama City on the Pacific coast.

Panama became a vital base for the Spanish, and many further expeditions set off from there. After the defeat of the Inca Empire at Cuzco in 1532, vast amounts of gold and silver were transported from Peru to Panama and then shipped back to Spain. The Spanish also built a road across the isthmus. Treasure and spices from the Spanish fleets in the Pacific were carried over this road to ships on the Caribbean coast and then transported to Spain.

*This engraving shows Christopher Columbus meeting Indians on his first voyage in 1492-93.*

## "NEW SPAIN"

There were several Spanish expeditions to the Yucatan, farther north, before Hernan Cortes landed in Mexico in 1519. Within two years, Cortes had conquered the mighty Aztec Empire and declared Mexico part of "New Spain." The Viceroyalty of New Spain was officially established in 1535. Like Panama in the south, Mexico became an important starting point for Spanish expeditions.

In 1523, Pedro de Alvarado set out to explore the lands south of Mexico. He

## THE PEOPLE OF NEW SPAIN

Early in the Spanish conquest of the Americas, Spanish ships carried only men to the New World. Many Spanish conquistadors and settlers married Indian women. Their children (of mixed Spanish and Indian heritage) became known as "mestizos." But later, when Spanish women arrived, a distinction grew between people of white skin who were born in Spain (the "peninsulares") and those who were born in the Spanish colonies, known as "criollos," or creoles. Another major group, the black Africans, arrived as slaves to work in the Spanish plantations and mines. By the end of the Colonial period, about one-third of the population of Central America was made up of mestizos and people of black African descent—known as ladinos. Indians made up about 65 percent of the population; white Spanish and creoles made up only 4 percent.

eventually defeated the Indians of Guatemala and pushed into El Salvador. In Nicaragua, however, a rival Spanish expedition sent from Panama by Pedrarias Davila stopped his advance. By the middle of the 16th century, the Spanish had established the Kingdom of Guatemala as part of the Viceroyalty of New Spain. The kingdom included modern Costa Rica, Nicaragua, El Salvador, Honduras, Guatemala, Belize, and the southern part of Mexico (Chiapas). Panama, however, was included in the Viceroyalty of Peru.

## DISEASE AND RELIGION

The Spanish invasions devastated the Indian peoples. The conquistadors brought diseases, such as smallpox and measles, that were previously unknown in the Americas. With no immunity to these infections, millions of Indians died. The Spanish also imposed their own religion, Roman Catholicism. Temples and other holy places were destroyed and replaced with Christian churches. The Roman Catholic Church became a powerful force in Central America.

*This 16th-century church at El Paraios was one of the first built by the Spanish in Honduras.*

**THE COLONIAL PERIOD**

**1492** First voyage of Columbus

**1501** Rodrigo de Bastidas explores coast of Panama

**1502** Columbus explores coast of Honduras, Nicaragua, Costa Rica, and Panama and claims

the region for Spain

**1513** Balboa's expedition; first Europeans to see the Pacific Ocean

**1517** Francisco Hernandez de Cordoba lands in the Yucatan

**1519** Pedrarias Davila founds Panama City

**1519–21** Hernan Cortes defeats the Aztec Empire

**1520s** Spain claims region of Belize

**1535** Viceroyalty of New Spain (Mexico)

established

**1544** Viceroyalty of Peru established

**1570** Spain establishes Audiencia (royal court) of Guatemala in Antigua; Nicaragua comes under the control of Audiencia

13

# THE ROAD TO INDEPENDENCE

**I**n 1808, Napoleon Bonaparte, the emperor of France, invaded Spain and installed his brother, Joseph, as king. The European conflict that followed weakened Spanish control in Central America.

## REVOLUTION IN SPAIN

The Spanish people rebelled against Joseph Bonaparte and demanded that King Ferdinand be restored to the throne. From 1808 to 1814, Spain was joined by Portugal and Britain in a war (the Peninsular War) to drive out the French. During this time, liberals in Spain drew up a new constitution that kept the monarchy but reduced the power of the Catholic Church.

The upheaval in Spain weakened Spanish control of its American colonies. While some conservatives in New Spain remained loyal to the Spanish throne, many liberals saw an opportunity to break away from colonial control.

*Joseph Bonaparte (1768–1844) was made king of Spain in 1808 by his brother, Napoleon.*

The Peninsular War ended in 1814 with the defeat of the French. King Ferdinand VII was restored to the Spanish throne. He quickly threw out the new constitution and tried to bring Spain's colonies back under control. In 1820, however, the Spanish army mutinied, and Ferdinand was forced to accept the constitution of 1812. This finally pushed Central America into independence.

In Mexico, rebels had been fighting for independence since 1810. In 1821, they were joined by a creole general named Agustin de Iturbide, who drew up the Plan of Iguala. Under this plan, Mexico would become an independent monarchy, headed by a ruler from the Spanish royal family.

### BELIZE

Although Spain claimed the region that is now Belize, the earliest European settlers were British. The first British settlement was established in 1638, and more British settlers arrived after 1665, attracted by logwood cutting (logwood was used to produce dyes for textiles). The Spanish frequently attacked the British settlements, which they considered illegal. The turning point came in 1798, when the British won a naval battle against a Spanish force, and British control in the area increased. Both Guatemala and Mexico also had claims on Belize, but in 1862, Britain declared it a colony (called British Honduras). It became independent in 1981. Guatemala, however, has never given up its claims to territory in Belize. Since independence, tensions between the two countries have continued.

## INDEPENDENCE

Mexico became independent in August 1821. The following month, all of the provinces of the Kingdom of Guatemala (see page 13) except El Salvador issued a declaration of independence from Spanish rule. Panama also declared independence in 1821 and became a province of Colombia (which had been independent since 1819). In January 1822, the Central American isthmus north of Panama (aside from El Salvador) was declared part of Mexico. Iturbide quickly sent a Mexican army to

*This engraved scene shows the streets of Mexico City when independence was proclaimed in 1821.*

bring El Salvador back into line. No member of the Spanish royal family ever ruled Mexico. It was Iturbide himself who took the title of Emperor Agustin I, but his reign was short-lived. After a military coup, Mexico was finally proclaimed a republic in 1823. The other Central American states then broke away from Mexico. At a congress in June 1823, these states established the United Provinces of Central America.

## THE ROAD TO INDEPENDENCE

**1808** Napoleon Bonaparte invades Spain and puts his brother Joseph on the Spanish throne

**1808–14** Spain, Portugal, and Britain fight France in the Peninsular War

**1810** Miguel Hidalgo starts a Mexican revolt

against the Spanish

**1814** France defeated in the Peninsular War

**February 24, 1821** Agustin de Iturbide issues the Plan of Iguala; **August 24** Mexico becomes independent; **September 15** The provinces of the

Kingdom of Guatemala (except El Salvador) declare independence from Spanish rule

**1822** Iturbide is proclaimed Emperor Agustin I of Mexico

**March 19, 1823** Abdication of Agustin I of Mexico; **June 24** United Provinces of

Central America established; **August 1** Mexico recognizes United Provinces of Central America

**1862** Belize becomes the colony of British Honduras

**1871** British Honduras becomes a Crown Colony

# GUATEMALA

**F**rom the start, the United Provinces of Central America was torn by disagreements between conservatives and liberals. The liberals gained the upper hand in the early years, but their reforms led to revolts by conservative supporters.

## Jose Rafael Carrera

In 1837, Jose Rafael Carrera, a "ladino" from Guatemala, led a successful Indian uprising, which soon brought about the end of the United Provinces. Guatemala became fully independent in 1839, and Carrera ruled as a conservative dictator from 1844 until his death in 1865, although he spent three of those years (1848-51) in exile. Carrera reestablished many of the privileges and powers of the Roman Catholic Church that had been removed under the previous liberal rule.

## Liberal Rule

The liberals returned to power in Guatemala in 1871, with Miguel Garcia Granados in charge. He restricted the power of the Church again, and this policy was enforced even more thoroughly by his successor, Justo Rufino Barrios, who was president from 1873 to 1885. Barrios modernized the country and promoted economic development, especially coffee growing. He seized church land and sold it for commercial coffee production. Barrios also forced peasant farmers to give up their land for coffee plantations, on which the farmers then worked as laborers.

## UFCO

The longest-serving of the liberal dictators who ruled Guatemala until 1944 was Manuel Estrada Cabrera, who was president from 1898 to 1920. During Cabrera's time in office, the United Fruit Company (UFCO)

### LIBERALS AND CONSERVATIVES

After independence, the ruling class in Central America was almost entirely creole. Politically, it was divided between conservatives and liberals. Many conservatives were wealthy creole landowners who wanted to retain certain aspects of the Colonial period—for example, the power and privileges of the Roman Catholic Church. They were deeply suspicious of the reforms proposed by the liberals. The liberals took their lead from the liberal revolt in Spain (see left). Their supporters were mainly non-landowning creoles, as well as white and ladino professionals. Liberal beliefs included abolishing slavery, restricting Church power, and granting rights and freedom of speech to all citizens.

was established in Guatemala. UFCO was formed in 1899 in the U.S. In the early years of the 20th century, the Cabrera government granted UFCO rights over large areas of land for banana plantations. UFCO was also given control of the construction and operation of railways.

In 1931, Jorge Ubico became president. During the 1920s, there had been protests and strikes by workers against UFCO and the railway companies. Ubico clamped down on these protests and introduced a secret police force to persecute anyone who opposed his rule. At the same time,

Not surprisingly, Arbenz's policy of taking over privately owned land and redistributing it among landless peasants met with great opposition from UFCO.

## U.S. Involvement

In 1954, fears about the damage being done to American companies in Guatemala led the U.S. government to intervene.

The U.S. used concerns about communist influences in the Arbenz government as an excuse to overthrow it. In June 1954, U.S.-backed rebels attacked Guatemala from a base in Honduras. Arbenz was forced to resign and went into exile. Colonel Carlos Castillo Armas, supported by the U.S., became president. He reversed most of the reforms introduced by Arevalo and Arbenz and persecuted communist supporters in Guatemala.

*Jorge Ubico (1878–1946) was elected democratically but assumed dictatorial powers once in office.*

he gave more concessions to UFCO. During World War II, Guatemala supported the U.S. Protests against Ubico continued, however, and in 1944, he was forced to resign. A military uprising in October 1944 led to the drawing up of a new, democratic constitution, and 10 years of social and economic revolution then followed.

## Land Reforms

Under President Juan Jose Arevalo (in power 1945-50), more people were given the right to vote, trade unions were strengthened, and a social security system was established for poor families. Arevalo's successor, Jacobo Arbenz Guzman, introduced land reforms in 1952. About 2 percent of the population controlled 74 percent of Guatemala's farming land, and UFCO had a monopoly on banana production.

*Carlos Castillo Armas suppressed labor movements and agricultural reform. He was murdered in 1957.*

## CIVIL WAR

In the years that followed, civil war tore Guatemala apart as left-wing rebels fought to restore the reforms they had lost, and a series of right-wing military governments put down the uprisings mercilessly. In particular, the Indian populations in the highlands suffered from the army's violence, and many thousands were killed.

In 1976, a huge earthquake devastated Guatemala. More than 27,000 people died, and more than a million lost their homes. In the aftermath, the government responded to guerrilla activity with terrible violence and ordered the massacres of whole villages that were suspected of sheltering rebels. In 1982, the guerrilla organizations united to form the National Revolutionary Union of Guatemala (URNG). In 1985, Vinicio Cerezo Arevalo became the first democratically elected president of Guatemala in nearly 20 years. He began talks between the government and the URNG, but the violence continued. A peace agreement between the government and the URNG was finally signed in 1996.

## FACING UP TO THE PAST

In the 1999 elections, Alfonso Portillo of the right-wing Guatemalan Republican Front (FRG) defeated Oscar Berger, the representative of the center parties. That same year, a United Nations investigation into Guatemala's civil war estimated that 200,000 people had been killed, mostly by

*Troops take to the streets of Guatemala City as civil unrest spreads in 1982.*

the security forces. Many of these atrocities happened in the early 1980s, during General Efrain Rios Montt's time in office.

In 2003, Montt ran for president but was heavily defeated. A year later, he was placed under house arrest in connection with the death of a journalist during the elections. It is hard to predict if he will ever face charges relating to the atrocities of the 1980s.

*Former Guatemala City Mayor Oscar Berger was elected president in 2003.*

## FACT FILE: GUATEMALA

**Population:** 12.3 million (2003)
**Capital:** Guatemala City
**Size:** 42,040 square miles (108,890 sq km)
**Ethnic makeup:** Indian 60%, mestizo 30%, others 10%
**Note:** Ladinos make up about 40% of the population. They include people of white, Indian, and mixed race origin who share a common Central American culture but speak Spanish and wear Western clothes.
**Religion:** Roman Catholic, Protestant, and local Mayan beliefs
**Official language:** Spanish, but more than 20 Mayan languages are also spoken
**Economy:** Tourism is very important; main exports are coffee, sugar, bananas, cardamom, fruit, vegetables, and meat.

## THE FUTURE

The eventual winner of the 2003 elections was a wealthy businessman named Oscar Berger, who represents the conservative center parties in Guatemala. Upon his election, Berger promised a major drive against corruption. He has also been responsible for organizing new investment in the economy. His first priority is to bring peace to his country and to ensure equality of opportunity, as well as basic human rights. It is a difficult challenge for his government.

**GUATEMALA**

**1906** First banana plantations developed by UFCO

**1920s** Strikes and protests against UFCO

**1931–44** Regime of dictator Jorge Ubico

**1939–45** World War II

**June 1944** Ubico resigns; **October 20** Military uprising

**1945–50** Presidency of Juan Jose Arevalo; new constitution and reforms

**1950–54** Presidency of Jacobo Arbenz Guzman; land reforms

**1954** U.S. backs invasion; Arbenz resigns; Colonel Carlos Castillo Armas becomes president; civil war follows

**1957** Castillo Armas assassinated

**1976** Earthquake devastates country

**1980s** Death squads kill thousands

**1982** Rebels unite as URNG

**1982–83** General Efrain Rios Montt seizes power

**1985** Vinicio Cerezo Arevalo elected

**1990** Jorge Serrano Elias becomes president

**1996** Government and URNG agree to peace

**1999** Alfonso Portillo wins elections

**2003** Oscar Berger wins elections

**2004** Montt arrested

# EL SALVADOR

**W**hen the Central American states broke from Spain in the 19th century, El Salvador resisted becoming part of Mexico. It joined the United Provinces of Central America, but when this union began to break up, it withdrew. It became independent in 1841.

*El Salvador relies heavily on coffee exports. Here, workers bag raw beans for processing.*

### THE FOURTEEN FAMILIES

After independence, El Salvador experienced great political instability. Presidents were overthrown, and powerful outsiders, such as Rafael Carrera of Guatemala, installed their own leaders in El Salvador. In the 1880s, laws were passed to prevent the Indian population from owning and farming communal land. Ownership of this land was taken over by a tiny but powerful group of people known as the "Fourteen Families" (although there were many more than 14). Coffee quickly became the most important crop because of its export potential.

### FACT FILE: EL SALVADOR

**Population:** 6.5 million (2003)
**Capital:** San Salvador
**Size:** 8,120 square miles (21,040 sq km)
**Ethnic makeup:** mostly mestizo, Indian 5–10%, white 1%
**Religion:** mostly Roman Catholic
**Official language:** Spanish
**Economy:** Coffee and sugar are the main exports; also soya, shrimp, tropical and ornamental flowers.

BELIZE

ONDURAS

NICAR

STA RICA

## PROFIT AND LOSS

In the early decades of the 20th century, El Salvador's economy flourished, almost entirely because of its coffee exports. But the country's wealth was held by a tiny number of rich and powerful landowners, while the vast majority of peasants worked on the coffee plantations and lived in great poverty.

In the late 1920s, a worldwide economic depression caused the price of coffee to drop. As their profits sank, landowners in El Salvador cut the wages of their peasant workers, which sparked a series of strikes. When the army seized power and installed a right-wing dictator, General Maximiliano Hernandez Martinez, the peasants rose in revolt. Martinez's reply was ferocious. Between 10,000 and 20,000 Indians were massacred as entire villages were destroyed and their inhabitants killed.

## MILITARY RULE

Martinez stayed in power until 1944, when he was overthrown, but the military kept control of El Salvador through a series of coups until the 1970s. In the late 1970s, widespread protests against the military government occurred, backed by the Roman Catholic Church. In 1979, a group of army officers seized power and set up a new government run by a junta (council) of both military officers and civilians. The junta promised to introduce reforms. When this did not happen, opposition groups and unions joined to form the Democratic Revolutionary Front (FDR).

## CIVIL WAR

In March 1980, Archbishop Oscar Arnulfo Romero, an outspoken supporter of the opposition groups, was shot by right-wing extremists while he was leading a service in the cathedral in the capital, San Salvador.

## THE "SOCCER WAR"

In 1969, Honduras and El Salvador played each other in the third round of the soccer World Cup. El Salvador won the game, but the violence surrounding the match led the two countries into a brief, four-day war. The issues behind the war, however, went much deeper than the soccer match. Since the 1920s, poor peasants had moved from El Salvador to Honduras in search of land. In 1969, Honduras expelled thousands of these illegal immigrants and redistributed the land among Hondurans.

The government in El Salvador did not welcome the immigrants' return, and after the match, it sent troops to invade Honduras. After four days of fighting, the two sides agreed to a ceasefire, but tensions continued. A peace agreement was finally signed in 1980.

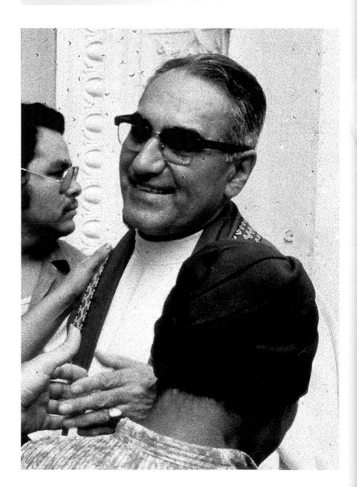

*Archbishop Oscar Arnulfo Romero (1917–80) was murdered by right-wing extremists.*

Later in the year, several more leading reformers were assassinated by government forces. In December, the junta appointed Christian democrat leader Jose Napoleon Duarte as president, but many people now believed that violence was the only way forward. Guerrilla forces of the Farabundo Marti National Liberation Front (FMLN) began to fight the government. The country sank into a bitter civil war.

Throughout the 1980s, Duarte's rule was strongly backed by the U.S., which sent millions of dollars in economic and military aid to help the fight against the left-wing guerrillas of the FMLN. Many people criticized U.S. support of a regime with such an appalling human rights record. Despite some government attempts at reform, the gulf between rich and poor remained as wide as ever. President Duarte tried to negotiate with the FMLN in 1986, but the civil war continued. Peasants were often the innocent victims of violence between the two sides. By 1989, it is estimated that about 70,000 people had died in the fighting. An earthquake that devastated the country in 1986 also left more than 1,000 people dead, and many thousands more lost their homes.

In 1989, support for the right-wing Nationalist Republican Alliance (ARENA) party led to the election of Alfredo Cristiani as president. Later that year, the FMLN staged attacks across the country, and fierce fighting broke out in San Salvador and other cities. The United Nations organized peace talks between the FMLN and ARENA, and

*Government troops round up suspected guerrillas in 1984 during El Salvador's civil war.*

*Jose Napoleon Duarte, photographed during the 1989 election campaign.*

next elections, internal divisions had weakened it. Once again, an ARENA candidate, Francisco Flores, was elected president. In 2001, more earthquakes killed 1,200 people and made a million homeless. A severe drought that same year caused drastic food shortages. The 2004 elections gave the fourth win in a row to ARENA, with Elias Antonio Saca, a young and popular journalist, as president. He has promised to end the country's violence and improve the economy.

after many failed attempts, the talks finally succeeded in January 1992. The peace agreement included reducing the size of the army, which had become very powerful as a result of U.S. backing. The FMLN also agreed to disarm, and in December 1992, it became a legal political party.

## ARENA VICTORIES

Although elections held in 1994 produced victory for ARENA, the FMLN was established as the second most powerful political party in the country. But by the

*Broadcaster Elias Antonio Saca, a descendant of Palestinian immigrants, became president in 2004.*

**EL SALVADOR**

**1920s** Depression leads to slump in coffee prices

**1931–44** Regime of Maximiliano Martinez

**1932** Peasant revolt put down; troops kill between 10,000 and 20,000 people

**1969** "Soccer War" with Honduras

**1979** Army officers seize power and install military/civilian junta; Democratic Revolutionary Front (FDR) founded

**March 1980** Murder of Archbishop Oscar Arnulfo Romero; **December** Jose Napoleon Duarte becomes president of ruling junta

**1981** Fighting escalates into civil war

**1984** Duarte elected president

**1986** Earthquake kills more than 1,000 and leaves thousands homeless

**1989** Alfredo Cristiani elected president

**1992** Ceasefire and

peace agreement

**1993** United Nations report on human rights abuses

**1998** Hurricane Mitch hits El Salvador

**1999** Francisco Flores elected president

**2004** Elias Antonio Saca elected president

23

# HONDURAS

When the United Provinces of Central America broke up, Honduras was the least-developed country in the region. General Francisco Morazan tried to rebuild the union between the countries, but this dream ended with his execution in 1842.

## GENERAL FRANCISCO MORAZAN

Francisco Morazan was born in 1792 in Tegucigalpa, Honduras. When Central America broke from Spain in 1821, Morazan resisted Honduras becoming part of Mexico. In 1823, he represented Honduras in establishing the United Provinces of Central America, and he became General Secretary in the Honduran government in 1824. When Jose Justo Milla tried to seize power in 1827, Morazan's forces defeated him. Morazan also defeated conservative rebels in El Salvador, and his fame spread throughout Central America. In 1830, as President of Central America, he introduced liberal reforms, such as freedom of speech and the right to divorce. This was fiercely opposed by conservatives and the Roman Catholic Church. When the United Provinces ended, Morazan went into exile in Colombia. He tried to reestablish a united Central America in 1842 but was captured and executed.

*Banana production is extremely important to the economy of Honduras.*

## BANANA REPUBLIC

Honduras is very mountainous, and communication is difficult. Mining for minerals such as silver and gold was developed during the 19th century, and some coffee was grown. But there was little economic or agricultural development until the 1890s, when companies from the U.S. developed banana plantations on the northern coast of Honduras. They also built railways and ports in exchange for more land and tax concessions. The three main companies were the Standard Fruit Company, Cuyamel, and the United Fruit Company (UFCO). By the end of the 1920s, Honduras was the biggest exporter of bananas in the world. The importance of bananas to the country's economy made the three U.S. companies very powerful in the political life of Honduras. It also inspired the term "banana republic," which was first used about Honduras.

## POLITICAL HISTORY

Since independence, the political history of Honduras has been one of frequent government changes, civil wars, and revolutions. In 1932, General Tiburcio Carias Andino of the National Party was elected president. He held power for 16 years—the longest period under the same regime since independence. During this time, the armed forces in Honduras set up training schools and military academies, partly paid for by the U.S.

In 1957, the power of the military was demonstrated when three army officers overthrew the president and called for new elections. The elections were won by Ramon Villeda Morales, a liberal, but military officers were suspicious of his reforms. In 1963, they overthrew him and installed Colonel Oswaldo Lopez Arellano as president. In 1969, Honduras went to war briefly with El Salvador (see page 21), which caused long-term tensions.

## HONDURAS AND THE U.S.

The armed forces governed Honduras until 1981, when Roberto Suazo Cordova of the Liberal Party was elected president. Nevertheless, the military continued to be extremely powerful throughout the 1980s. Many left-wing opponents of the government were imprisoned without trial during this time, and it is likely that death squads killed many others.

During the early 1980s, Honduras became entangled in the politics of neighboring Nicaragua. The U.S. wanted to weaken the Sandinista government in Nicaragua, so it secretly backed the Nicaraguan Contra rebel movement (see pages 30-31). In return for large amounts of economic aid, Honduras agreed to help the U.S.

*Honduran soldiers carry out surveillance on the border between Honduras and Nicaragua in 1986.*

The Honduran government allowed Contra attacks to be launched from their territory and provided base camps and airfields for the Contra rebels to use.

## MILITARY POWER

In 1989, the Central American Peace Plan brought an end to the civil war in Nicaragua. The last Contra rebels left Honduras the following year. Civilian government remained in Honduras throughout the 1990s, with elections every four years, but the armed forces continued to be a powerful presence. For example, when the government tried to investigate alleged human rights abuses by the armed forces, the military sent tanks into the Honduran capital, Tegucigalpa. In the late 1990s, however, control of the police and the armed forces finally passed from the military to the civilian government.

Sadly, basic human rights are still frequently abused, and investigations of these abuses are hampered or blocked.

## HURRICANE MITCH

In 1998, a tropical storm called Hurricane Mitch swept across Honduras. The violent weather devastated much of the country,

*Hurricane Mitch caused massive devastation to Central America in 1998.*

## STREET CHILDREN

Since 2000, more than 1,500 children and young people have died on the streets of the cities of Honduras. Many have been killed in gang violence, often linked to drugs. But it is alleged that at least 10 percent of those found dead were murdered by death squads set up by the police and the army. The United Nations says these murders are part of an unofficial policy to "cleanse" the city streets of the poor. When Ricardo Maduro became president in 2002, he promised to deal with the street violence. The following year, the government announced its intention to set up a commission to look into the murders. But the deaths continue, and violence between gangs of street youths (known as "maras") is a growing problem.

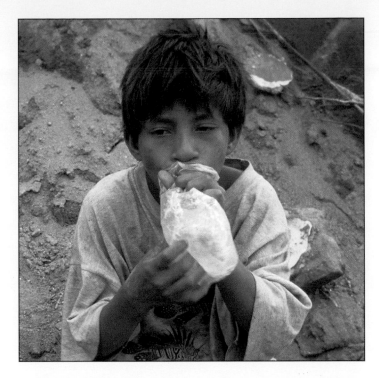

*A street child in Tegucigalpa inhales glue from a bag.*

and at least 5,600 people died. Thousands more were injured. The storm caused damage estimated at more than $3 billion, including the destruction of three-quarters of the banana crop. This dealt a severe blow to the economic development of the country.

As Honduras enters the 21st century, huge inequalities still remain between the poverty-stricken majority and the tiny minority who are wealthy. Most people in Honduras still struggle against the continuing effects of poverty, lack of food, and fear of disease. In addition, the sale and use of illegal drugs has caused a huge rise in violent crime, which mostly affects young people (see box above).

**HONDURAS**

**1842** Execution of General Francisco Morazan

**1899** Founding of Standard Fruit Company and United Fruit Company

**1911** Founding of Cuyamel Fruit Company

**1932** General Tiburcio Carias Andino is elected president

**1957** Elections won by Ramon Villeda Morales

**1963** Colonel Oswaldo Lopez Arellano leads coup and seizes power

**1969** "Soccer War" with El Salvador

**1980s** Human rights abuses against opposition members

**1981** End of military government as Roberto Suazo Cordova becomes president

**1982** U.S.-backed Contra rebels launch attacks against Nicaragua from Honduran territory

**1989** Civil war in Nicaragua ends

**1990** Last Contra rebels leave Honduras; Rafael Callejas becomes president

**1993** Carlos Reina elected president; commission set up to investigate human rights abuses by military

**1997** Carlos Flores elected president

**1998** Police come under civilian control; Hurricane Mitch devastates country

**1999** Armed forces come under civilian control

**2000s** Rise in street crime; murder of street children continues

# NICARAGUA

**W**hen Nicaragua became independent in 1838, a fierce rivalry existed between the two main cities that had been founded by the Spanish—Granada and Leon. Granada was a conservative stronghold, while Leon was the base of the liberals.

## WILLIAM WALKER

After independence, fierce fighting broke out between the two sides for control of the country. In 1855, the liberals invited William Walker, an adventurer from the U.S., to help them in their struggle against the conservatives. Walker arrived with a small band of followers and captured Granada in a surprise attack. However, Walker himself then seized power and was elected president in 1856. A coalition of Central American states managed to drive Walker out, and in 1857, Nicaragua came under conservative rule. Walker attempted to reenter Nicaragua several times but was captured and finally executed in Honduras in 1860.

*William Walker was elected president in 1856.*

## NICARAGUA AND THE U.S.

Because of its geographical location, Nicaragua was of great interest to powerful countries such as Great Britain and the U.S throughout the 19th century. These countries wanted to build a canal across Central America to create a direct shipping route between the Atlantic and Pacific Oceans. Nicaragua seemed to be a good choice for this massive project because Lake Nicaragua and the San Juan River already provided a navigable route across much of the isthmus. Britain claimed most of the Atlantic coastline of Nicaragua but finally gave up its claim in 1894. The U.S., however, wanted to control the inland area through which any canal would pass.

In 1893, General Jose Santos Zelaya led a liberal revolt in Nicaragua and seized power as dictator. The U.S. government viewed Zelaya's takeover with great suspicion. In 1909, when the chance came to support conservative rebels in an attempt to remove him, the U.S. did exactly that. Chaos followed, and the new president, Adolfo Diaz, was forced to ask the U.S. for military aid to try to prevent civil war. In 1912, U.S. troops arrived in Nicaragua. The U.S. also pledged financial help and provided massive loans from American banks. In return, these banks effectively took over control of Nicaragua's national bank and its railway system.

## AUGUSTO CESAR SANDINO

U.S. troops left Nicaragua in 1925, but civil war between liberal and conservative factions soon broke out. The troops returned the following year to restore peace, and in 1927, an agreement was signed between the two sides. Under this agreement, the police force and army were disbanded and replaced

*A Nicaraguan women's regiment commanded by the wives of two generals was among those opposing U.S. and government forces in 1928.*

with a National Guard that had been trained in the U.S. One liberal leader, Augusto Cesar Sandino, refused to sign the agreement while the U.S. still had a military presence in Nicaragua. Sandino and a band of followers established hideouts in the mountains. They began a guerrilla war against the U.S. troops and the National Guard, who tried unsuccessfully to hunt them down.

## THE SOMOZA FAMILY

Convinced that its involvement had brought economic and political stability, the U.S. withdrew its troops from Nicaragua in 1933. The National Guard was commanded by Anastasio Somoza Garcia, who ordered the murder of Sandino in 1934 and, in 1936,

### FACT FILE: NICARAGUA

**Population:** 5.4 million (2003)
**Capital:** Managua
**Size:** 50,000 square miles (129,495 sq km)
**Ethnic makeup:** mestizo 69%, white 14%, black 9%, Indian 5%, mixed black-Indian 3%
**Religion:** Roman Catholic
**Official language:** Spanish
**Economy:** Nicaragua is one of the world's poorest countries. Main exports are beef, coffee, sugar, bananas, and seafood.

also forced the president, Juan Sacasa, to resign. The following year, Somoza himself became president. This began more than 40 years of rule by Somoza and his family. Anastasio Somoza was assassinated in 1956, and his son Luis replaced him as president. Another son, Anastasio Somoza Debayle, then held the presidency from 1967 until he was overthrown in 1979.

## THE SANDINISTAS

The Somozas tried to improve the Nicaraguan economy while becoming extremely rich themselves. They cooperated closely with the U.S. and received aid from successive American governments. But the regime was a dictatorship, and guerrilla warfare was to become the opposition's main means of effective resistance. Several guerrilla groups had combined to form the Sandinista National Liberation Front in 1961; by 1978, conflict between the Sandinistas and the military had developed into civil war. Somoza was overthrown and forced into exile in 1979. He was assassinated in 1980.

The Sandinistas took power with a junta (military council). Their leader, Daniel Ortega Saavedra, was elected president in 1984. The Sandinistas claimed the Somoza family estates (about 20 percent of all farming land in the country) and turned them into state farms. They aimed to create

*A group of well-equipped Sandinista soldiers, 1986.*

## DANIEL ORTEGA SAAVEDRA

Daniel Ortega Saavedra was born in La Libertad, Nicaragua, in 1946. In 1963, he joined the Sandinista National Liberation Front (FSLN), eventually becoming head of urban resistance. He was arrested and imprisoned in 1967 but was released in an exchange deal in 1974. In July 1979, after Somoza Debayle fled to the U.S., Ortega joined the "Junta for National Reconstruction."

In 1984, FSLN won elections, and the following year, Ortega became president of Nicaragua. However, Contra rebels, who were funded by the U.S., refused to accept his election. In the 1990 elections, the FSLN lost to the National Opposition Union (UNO), and Ortega was replaced as president by Violetta Chamorro. Ortega and the FSLN lost elections in 1996 and 2001.

a mixed economy, with both public and private ownership, and started to improve healthcare and literacy.

## THE CONTRAS AND THE SANDINISTAS

With the Sandinistas in charge, relations between Nicaragua and the U.S. broke down. The Sandinistas had close links with the communist regime in Cuba. Alarmed by this, and claiming that the Sandinistas supplied arms to rebel groups in other Central American countries, the U.S. stopped aid payments to Nicaragua in 1981. The U.S. also assisted opponents of the Sandinista government—former members of the National Guard, who became known as "Contras." Beginning in 1982, the Contras launched attacks on Nicaragua from bases in Honduras (see pages 25-26). In 1984, the U.S. helped the Contras put explosive mines in several Nicaraguan harbors—an action condemned as illegal by the International Court of Justice.

In 1985, the U.S. imposed an embargo on Nicaragua, which ended trade between the two countries.

In 1987, the Sandinista government and the Contras met to try to agree to the terms of a peace plan. The plan had been drawn up by Oscar Arias Sanchez, the president of Costa Rica. The two sides reached an agreement and signed a ceasefire in 1988. American aid to the Contras ended in 1989, and the organization gradually fell apart. The Contras finally disbanded and left their bases in Honduras in 1990.

*"We grew up in a situation where we didn't know what freedom or justice were, and therefore we didn't know what democracy was."*

**Daniel Ortega Saavedra**

## DEFORESTATION IN NICARAGUA

About 40 percent of Nicaragua is covered by rain forest, but this percentage has been shrinking as the forest is exploited, mainly by foreign companies. From 1945 to 1960, the U.S.-owned Nicaraguan Long Leaf Pine Company paid money directly to the Somoza family. In return, the company was allowed to cut down all of the commercially valuable trees in an area of 1,160 square miles (3,000 sq km) of rain forest in northeast Nicaragua. Vast forest areas were also lost to cotton plantations in the 1950s and to cattle ranching in the 1960s and '70s. Poverty has also played its part, because peasant families, forced from their land, had little choice but to clear plots in the forests to grow food crops. When the soil was exhausted, the peasants took new land. Cattle ranchers then claimed the land. In this way, peasants and ranchers moved deeper into the rain forests.

*Ranchers raise cattle where rain forest animals once lived.*

## THE CHAMORRO GOVERNMENT

Although the Contras lost their war against the Sandinistas, the cost of fighting the war, along with the U.S. trade embargo, devastated the Nicaraguan economy. The people of Nicaragua made their feelings clear in the 1990 elections. A coalition of 14 opposition parties, called the National Opposition Union (UNO), defeated the Sandinista party, which was under the leadership of Daniel Ortega.

The U.S. then lifted its trade embargo and promised aid for the war-torn country. But the new president, Violetta Barrios de Chamorro, faced huge problems. The Sandinistas were still a powerful force and controlled the armed forces and the trade unions. Chamorro's government did not have enough money to keep its promise to give land to former Contras. In the early 1990s, fighting broke out between the "recontras" and Sandinista sympathizers, but an agreement to end the fighting was reached in 1994.

Chamorro's government tried to improve Nicaragua's economy and introduced some constitutional reforms. These included reducing the length of presidential terms from six to five years and making it illegal for a president to be elected for a second successive term or to be succeeded by a close family relative. In the 1996 elections, Arnoldo Aleman Lacoyo of the right-wing Liberal Alliance defeated Ortega's party.

## HURRICANE MITCH

In 1998, Hurricane Mitch hit Nicaragua, causing massive devastation. The storm left nearly 3,000 dead and thousands homeless. It was a crippling blow to Nicaragua's fragile economy and caused terrible hardship across the country, made worse by droughts in the same year. Foreign aid helped to rebuild the shattered country, and the economy started to improve once more, but there were allegations of corruption against Aleman's government. The elections of 2001 saw Enrique Bolanos of the PLC defeat Ortega—the third election defeat in a row for the FSLN. Despite this, the Sandinistas voted for Ortega to continue to be their leader. Meanwhile, in 2003, former President Arnoldo Aleman was charged with corruption and jailed for a 20-year term.

In 2004, Nicaragua received the promise of financial help from the World Bank, which agreed to wipe out 80 percent of Nicaragua's $6.5 billion foreign debt. It also announced that it would be offering a $75 million loan to help reduce poverty in Nicaragua.

*Enrique Bolanos became president in 2001.*

President Bolanos said it was the best news for Nicaragua in the last 25 years.

---

**NICARAGUA**

**1894** Britain gives up the Atlantic coastline, and the Mosquito Coast is taken back by Nicaragua

**1909** Conservative revolt backed by U.S.

**1911** Loans negotiated with U.S.

**1912** U.S. troops sent to Nicaragua

**1925** Withdrawal of U.S. troops; civil war

**1926** U.S. troops return

**1927** Peace agreement between liberals and conservatives; guerrilla attacks led by Augusto Cesar Sandino

**1933** U.S. troops leave

**1934** Murder of Sandino

**1936** Somoza overthrows President Juan Sacasa

**1937** Somoza becomes president

**1956** Somoza assassinated; replaced as president by his son Luis

**1961** Formation of Sandanista National Liberation Front

**1978** Civil war

**1979** Overthrow of Somoza; Sandinistas install a junta

**1981** U.S. stops aid payments

**1982** First U.S.-backed Contra attacks

**1984** Daniel Ortega Saavedra is elected president

**1985** U.S. imposes trade embargo

**1988** Ceasefire signed between Sandanistas and Contras

**1990** Violetta Barrios de Chamorro of UNO wins elections; Contras disband and leave Honduras

**1998** Hurricane Mitch devastates the country

**2001** Enrique Bolanos of PLC wins elections

**2003** Aleman jailed

**2004** World Bank agrees to aid package

# COSTA RICA

**D**azzled by rumors of gold, the Spanish named the region Costa Rica, or "rich coast." But the area did not live up to its reputation, and at independence, it remained a remote and undeveloped part of New Spain.

## COFFEE AND BANANAS

Costa Rica became independent in 1838. After a decade of turbulence, Juan Rafael Mora began a 10-year term as president in 1849. By this time, coffee growing was already established in Costa Rica, and the government offered free grants of land to coffee growers. Many small, family-owned farms were established, and a prosperous middle-class developed. This was vital to the development of a politically and economically stable country.

In 1870, General Tomas Guardia seized power and ruled as a dictator. He used taxes from coffee production to finance the building of

*The Costa Rican capital of San José. It was covered by a 5-inch (13 cm) layer of mud after the volcano Irazu erupted in 1963.*

### FACT FILE: COSTA RICA

**Population:** 4.2 million (2003)
**Capital:** San José
**Size:** 19,730 square miles (51,100 sq km)
**Ethnic makeup:** mestizo and white 98%, in Limón area 33% black African, about 5,000 Indians
**Religion:** Roman Catholic and Protestant
**Official language:** Spanish
**Economy:** Main exports are coffee, beef, and bananas. Strong tourism industry.

railways and public buildings. One railway contract went to Minor C. Keith, an American businessman. Keith brought black Africans from the Caribbean to work as laborers, set up banana plantations on the east coast, and started the United Fruit Company. Bananas became as important as coffee to Costa Rica's economy.

## COSTA RICAN POLITICS

A system of democratic government developed in Costa Rica after 1889, with only a few interruptions. In 1948, when the results of elections were disputed, a brief period of fighting was followed by the installation of a junta (military council). Jose Figueres Ferrer, the new leader, drew up a new constitution that abolished the army, gave women the right to vote, and granted full citizenship to Costa Rica's black population. Figueres also founded the National Liberation Party (PLN) and was elected president in 1953. Since 1958, the PLN and its opposition parties have alternated in power.

## PEACE WORK

In the 1980s, the Costa Rican economy declined and unemployment grew. Another threat was the political instability of Costa Rica's neighbor, Nicaragua (see page 32). Both Contra rebels and Nicaraguan refugees entered Costa Rica, but President Oscar Arias Sanchez kept his country neutral.

*Oscar Arias Sanchez, president 1986–90.*

## CHALLENGE FOR THE FUTURE

The 1990s saw a continuation of the rivalry between Costa Rica's two main parties, the PLN and the main opposition party, the Social Christian Unity Party (PUSC; formed in 1985). Coffee and bananas remain the staples of the economy, although tourism is increasingly important. In elections held in 2002, Abel Pacecho of the conservative PUSC was eventually victorious after two rounds of voting. The main challenge for the future is to boost the economy despite a worldwide slump in coffee prices.

**COSTA RICA**

**1808** Introduction of coffee production to Costa Rica

**1838** Costa Rica becomes independent

**1874** Introduction of banana cultivation

**1889** Democratic government

**1917–19** Frederico Tinoco seizes power

**1948** Disputed election leads to six-week civil war

**1949** New liberal constitution drawn up under leadership of Jose Figueres Ferrer

**1952** Figueres founds National Liberation Party (PLN)

**1963–64** Eruption of volcano damages crops and buildings

**1985** Opposition parties unite to form Social Christian Unity Party (PUSC)

**1986** Oscar Arias Sanchez is elected president

**1987** Arias Sanchez wins Nobel Peace Prize

**2002** Abel Pacecho of PUSC elected president

# PANAMA

**W**hen Panama broke away from Spanish rule in 1821, it became part of Colombia. It remained a province of Colombia until 1903, although revolts against Colombian rule began as early as the 1830s.

## THE GOLD RUSH

In the late 1840s and 1850s, people from around the world rushed to the goldfields of California, hoping to make their fortunes. Reaching California was hard. Many eager prospectors came by ship to Colon, on the Caribbean side of Panama. They then made their way across the isthmus to Panama City and boarded ships to California. The difficult land journey was finally replaced by the first transcontinental railway in the Americas in the 1850s. Black laborers came to Panama from the Caribbean islands to work on the railway, and some settled in Panama.

*Passengers on board a steamer travel to California via Panama in 1849.*

## FACT FILE: PANAMA

**Population:** 3.1 million (2003)
**Capital:** Panama City
**Size:** 30,195 square miles (78,200 sq km)
**Ethnic makeup:** mestizo 60%, white 14%, black African 12%, Indian 8%, Asian 4%, others 2%
**Religion:** Roman Catholic
**Official language:** Spanish
**Economy:** Mainstay of the economy is the Panama Canal and services associated with it. Other sources of income include tourism and exports of bananas, shrimp, and copper.

## BUILDING A CANAL

The prospect of building a canal across Panama had been discussed since the 17th century. In the 1880s, the dream seemed likely to become a reality. The government of Colombia finally authorized a French company to start digging. The company's director, Ferdinand de Lesseps, had been responsible for the construction of the Suez Canal, which linked the Mediterranean and Red Seas. About 18 miles (30 km) of canal was dug in Panama before the company ran out of money in 1893, and work stopped. By then, more than 20,000 people had died of tropical diseases while working on the canal. The U.S. had been interested in building a canal across Nicaragua (see page 28). But in the early 20th century, the U.S. government decided to take over the abandoned Panama Canal instead.

*The Panama Canal opened for traffic in 1914. This photograph shows the SS Ancon, the first ship to sail through the canal.*

Backed by the U.S. Navy, the people of Panama declared their independence from Colombia in 1903. Despite protests from Colombia, the U.S. recognized the new republic and immediately struck a deal with the government of Panama. Under the terms of this treaty, the U.S. was given complete control of an area of Panama 10 miles (16 km) wide and 53 miles (85 km) long "in perpetuity" (forever), in which to construct the canal.

## THE CANAL ZONE

The canal opened on August 15, 1914, and immediately became a major international waterway. Life inside the Panama Canal Zone was one of privilege and wealth, and Colon and Panama City flourished from the trade brought by the canal. But most of the rest of the country remained poor, rural, and undeveloped.

Many ordinary Panamanians resented U.S. control of the Canal Zone and the higher wages paid to Americans who worked there. In 1964, anti-American feelings erupted into riots, and 23 Panamanians, as well as 4 U.S. soldiers, died.

## OMAR TORRIJOS HERRERA

In 1968, the chief of the National Guard, General Omar Torrijos Herrera, overthrew the president and installed a military junta (council) with himself as its leader. Torrijos ruled as a dictator, but he also negotiated a new treaty with the U.S. Signed in 1977, this treaty guaranteed an end to U.S. control of the Canal Zone. The U.S. agreed to transfer its ownership to Panama by the end of 1999 and to remove all of its military bases from the country.

## MILITARY RULE

Torrijos died in 1981, but the military junta continued to control Panamanian politics, and in 1983, General Manuel Antonio Noriega became head of the National Guard. Noriega built up both the armed forces and his own power over the political and economic life of Panama. In 1988, the U.S. accused Noriega of drug trafficking offenses and imposed harsh economic sanctions on Panama. The country quickly descended into chaos. In elections held in 1989, Guillermo Endara of the opposition "civic crusade" defeated Noriega's candidate. The military leaders immediately announced that the elections were invalid, and Noriega declared himself head of state.

## OPERATION "JUST CAUSE"

These events prompted the U.S. to intervene. In December 1989, American

President George Bush sent 20,000 troops to Panama to overthrow the Noriega regime. Noriega was captured and taken to the U.S. to stand trial for drug trafficking, and the opposition leader, Endara, was installed as president.

Endara began to dismantle the army and replace it with a police force, but he himself was accused of corruption. The 1994 elections brought victory for Ernesto Perez Balladares of the Democratic Revolutionary Party (PRD), Noriega's old party. Five years later, Maria Moscoso became Panama's first female president. In December 1999, she oversaw the return of the Canal Zone to Panamanian control.

## THE ROAD AHEAD

In the 21st century, Panama's economy has improved, and there has been an effort to

**GENERAL NORIEGA**

Manuel Antonio Noriega was born in Panama City in 1934. He received military training in Peru and the U.S., then joined Panama's National Guard. At first, he was a U.S. ally, paid by the Central Intelligence Agency (CIA) to provide secret intelligence. He took part in the coup that put Torrijos into power and became head of military intelligence in Panama. After Torrijos's death, Noriega promoted himself to general. He backed pro-U.S. forces in El Salvador and Nicaragua. In 1988, however, the U.S. withdrew its support and charged him with drug offenses. In 1989, Noriega was the prime target of operation "Just Cause." He took refuge in the Vatican embassy in Panama, where U.S. troops tried to break his spirit by playing continuous loud rock music outside the building. Noriega surrendered in 1990 and was tried in Miami. He was sentenced to 40 years in prison, which was reduced to 30 years in 1999.

investigate and deal with government corruption. Drug and arms smuggling across the border between Colombia and Panama remains a major problem, although Panama's police force recently captured the leader of one of Colombia's drug gangs. Colombia is a major producer of illegal drugs such as cocaine and heroin, most of which end up in the U.S.

*Police in Panama destroy packets of seized drugs, September 2000.*

In 2004, the presidential elections were won by Martin Torrijos, son of the former military leader. He has promised to eliminate poverty, corruption, and despair, and to establish opportunity and prosperity for all.

**PANAMA**

**1830** Panama becomes part of Colombia

**1853** Transcontinental railway opens across Panama

**1880s** French company starts work on the Panama Canal

**1893** Work stops on the Panama Canal as money runs out

**1903** Panama declares independence from Colombia; U.S. and Panama negotiate Canal Zone treaty

**1904** Work starts again on Canal

**1914** Opening of Panama Canal

**1939** Panama ceases to be U.S. Protectorate

**1964** Anti-U.S. riots in Panama

**1977** U.S. and Panama sign new treaty about Canal Zone

**1983** Noriega head of National Guard

**1988** Noriega accused of drug trafficking and other offenses

**1989** Elections declared invalid by Noriega; U.S. launches operation "Just Cause" to remove Noriega from power

**1990** Noriega arrested and tried in U.S.

**1994** Democratic Revolutionary Party (PRD) wins elections

**1999** Canal Zone handed back to Panama by U.S.

**2003** Panama celebrates centennial

**2004** Martin Torrijos wins presidential elections

# THE FUTURE

**I**n the 21st century, Central America is more politically stable than at any time since independence. But social inequality is still a huge issue, and poverty remains a major problem.

*Poverty is still a big problem in Central America. Here, Guatemalans pick through garbage to find items to sell so they can buy food to eat.*

It is estimated that half of the population of Central America—about 19 million people—lives in poverty. These people cannot afford basics such as food, housing, and clothes. They do not have access to a basic education, nor to healthcare, sanitation, and clean water. As in the past, the gap between rich and poor remains very wide. In Guatemala, for example, the richest 10 percent of the population continues to control almost half of the country's national income.

## FOREIGN DEBT
Natural disasters such as Hurricane Mitch, which hit Guatemala, Nicaragua, El Salvador, and Honduras in 1998, and the 2001 earthquakes in El Salvador have worsened the plight of the poor and devastated the economies of these countries. Although money has flowed into Central America from

## GANG CULTURE

Poverty, drugs, and lack of access to education and jobs have driven many young people in Central America into gang cultures. Such gangs are well organized and often extremely violent. In El Salvador, the problem has been made worse by the forced deportation of many immigrants from the U.S. back to their homeland. There are two main international gangs, the Mara Salvatrucha and the Mara 18. The local branches of these gangs are responsible for high levels of crime, such as kidnappings, murders, and the smuggling of drugs and arms. The response by the authorities has been a mixture of repression (rounding up and imprisoning gang members) and positive projects to try to convince people to leave the gangs.

*A policeman arrests a young gang member in El Salvador.*

sources such as the European Union and the U.S. to help with rebuilding, the amount of aid has been dwarfed by the money owed by the Central American countries as foreign debt. These debts date from the 1970s, when countries in Central America borrowed heavily. Some estimates put the total debt at around $35 billion. This means that while countries such as Guatemala and Nicaragua are struggling to find enough money to provide basic healthcare and education for their people, they are paying millions every day just to cover the interest on their debts.

Many people believe that the only way forward is for creditors to "forgive" the debts of the world's poorest countries. In 2004, the World Bank announced that it was canceling a large part of Nicaragua's foreign debt under its Heavily Indebted Poor Countries (HIPC) initiative. The HIPC program provides debt relief for countries that pursue sound economic policies and genuine measures to reduce poverty.

## CENTRAL AMERICAN TRADE

Since independence, the countries of Central America have built up economies based largely on the export of agricultural products, particularly coffee, bananas, and sugar. This makes them very vulnerable to changes in world prices for these commodities. Many countries have been trying to develop other products for export, such as shrimp or tropical flowers.

In 2004, the U.S. signed a Central American Free Trade Agreement with some countries. This removes tariffs that limited trade between the U.S. and other countries. It is part of a plan to set up a free trade area throughout the Americas. But opponents say the agreement will actually increase poverty. They argue that staple products such as rice, corn, and beans will be exported from the U.S., where they are subsidized, and sold at very low prices. Small Central American farmers will be unable to compete, so their livelihoods will be further undermined.

# GLOSSARY

**Assassinated** When a public or political figure is murdered, usually by a surprise attack.

**Aztec Empire** The empire that flourished in modern-day Mexico from the 15th century until it was overthrown by Cortes in the 16th century.

**Banana republic** A term used to describe a small country, particularly in Central America, that is often politically unstable and dependent on one commodity (such as bananas) for export.

**Civilian** Nonmilitary.

**Coalition** A temporary alliance between countries or groups of people for a specific reason.

**Colony** A territory ruled by a foreign power or state.

**Commodity** A product that can be traded.

**Concession** A grant of rights over land or property often given by a government to a company.

**Conquistador (conqueror)** The name given to the Spanish military adventurers who invaded the Americas in the 16th century.

**Conservative** In Central America, the conservatives were mainly landowners who wanted to keep aspects of the colonial era and were suspicious of reforms proposed by the liberals.

**Constitution** A written document that sets out the group of principles by which a country is governed.

**Coup** A sudden violent or illegal overthrow of an existing government.

**Creditor** Someone who is owed money.

**Creole** In Central America, people with white skin who were born in the Spanish colonies.

**Crown Colony** A colony directly controlled and administered by the British government.

**Democratic** Describes a political system in which the government is elected by all the people.

**Dictator** An absolute ruler, who is not restricted by a country's constitution or laws.

**Drug trafficking** The illegal trade in drugs.

**Embargo** An order to prevent something—for example, trade and commerce.

**Genocide** The policy of deliberately killing a particular group of people.

**Great Depression** The economic slump that affected countries around the world in the late 1920s and '30s.

**Guerrilla** A member of a rebel armed force who fights against regular forces such as the army or police.

**Human rights** The basic rights of a human being—for example, the right to freedom and justice.

**Illiteracy** The inability to read and write.

**Inca Empire** An empire that flourished in the Andean region of South America from the 15th century until its overthrow by Spanish conquistadors in the 16th century.

**Indigenous** Native to a particular place.

**Isthmus** A narrow strip of land connecting two larger areas of land.

**Junta** A military council.

**Ladinos** In Central America, the term used for mestizos and people of black African descent. In Guatemala, it describes people of white, Indian, and mixed origin who share a common Central American culture but speak Spanish and wear Western clothes.

**Liberals** In Central America, liberals believed in reforms such as restricting the power of the Church, individual rights, and freedom of speech.

**Maya** The dominant Indian culture from about A.D. 300 until 900 in an area that covered present-day Guatemala and Belize, the southern part of Mexico, and parts of El Salvador and Honduras.

**Mesoamerica (Middle America)** The name given to Mexico and Central America together.

**Mestizo** People of mixed Indian and European ancestry.

**Monopoly** Exclusive control over the right to sell a product.

**Republic** A country governed by an elected head of state called a president.

**Sanction** A measure agreed to by countries against another country that has broken international law.

**Security forces** A general term for the armed forces or police force.

**Subsidize** To support something or someone with financial aid.

**Tariff** A tax on imports, usually imposed in order to control the amount of a commodity entering a country.

**Vatican** The headquarters of the Roman Catholic Church in Rome.

**Yucatan** The peninsula that forms the southernmost part of Mexico and includes Belize and part of Guatemala.

# INDEX